The Awkward Years

64 Tips for Surviving High School

The Awkward Years

64 Tips for Surviving High School

Jenna Sundell

Independently Published

ISBN: 9781790190065

For my nieces and nephews

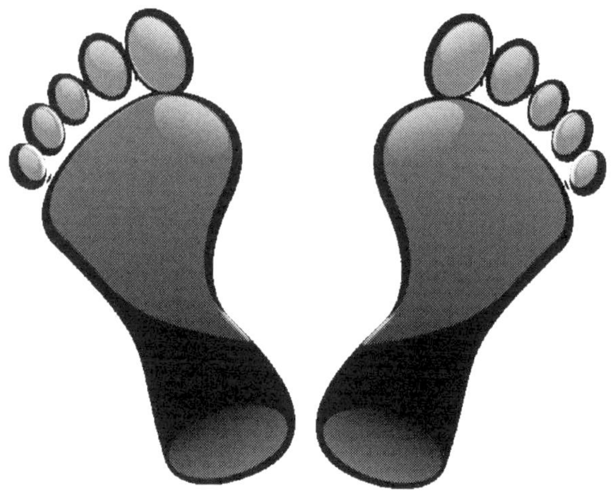

Author's Note

You stand at the mid-point between the innocent obliviousness of childhood and the responsible comprehension of adulthood. As a teenager, you still feel the magic of knowing anything is possible, yet you have begun to recognize the expansive effects of your actions. This is a powerful, confusing, overwhelming and awkward time. While in this transition time seems to crawl, later you'll see how fast the teen years whisk by. Tread lightly and treat yourself with compassionate care.

~ Jenna Sundell

Contents

Preface

As you read through these tips in whatever order you choose, stop to think about them and talk about them with your friends. You may want to read only a few at a time, and then consider what those ideas mean to you and how they are relevant to your life.

Pay close attention to any you don't agree with or don't understand. It can be fun to journal about your thoughts or discuss them with others to help make your insights clearer.

If there's a tip you find confusing or want to know more about, point it out to a parent or other trusted adult. Ask them to share their point of view with you. They may not have a complete answer to your questions, but together you can explore the possibilities.

1 – Firsts

We always remember our Firsts.

Because you'll remember, make sure you do it how, when, with whom, and in a way you'll want to remember. By making a conscious choice, you begin to learn how to claim your personal power.

ERRO

2 – Mistakes

No matter how old you are, it's always OK to make mistakes. The important thing is accepting that you made a mistake and doing what you can to make it right.

3 – Embarrassment

When you do something foolish or embarrassing, or just plain stupid in front of others, they may notice, but not for long.

Most people are very self-absorbed, so they will quickly forget about your drama in favor of one of their own.

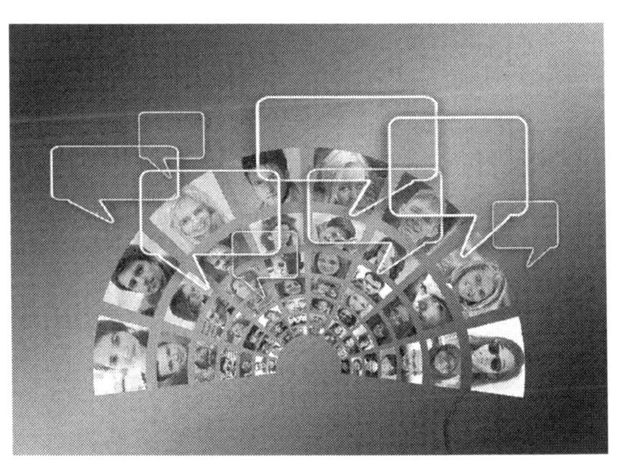

4 – Flexibility

During the teen years, your body and personality structure are completely fluid.

For most people, these years are when they are the most flexible both physically and mentally.

In other words, this is the easiest time for you to be whoever you want to be.

Try on different looks and personalities to see what feels right to you.

If you don't like it, you can always change by trying on something new.

5 – Freedom

This time of change and exploration is also a time of freedom. When people in their 30's and 40's alter their personality or mode of dress, their friends and family often become concerned that something is wrong. At 50, they call it a mid-life crisis.

When you do it as a teenager, people understand it as normal exploration. Enjoy the freedom to play at being whoever you want to be on any given day.

Under
Construction

6 – Rebuilding

Your body is rebuilding itself into a whole new form, one that will carry you for the rest of your life.

Because of this, it's a good idea to feed your body well, and be patient with it as it does its job.

7 – Create

Your mind is expanding and strengthening as you explore new views of yourself and the world around you.

Allow yourself to express what you're experiencing through art, music, and writing.

It doesn't matter if you or anyone else likes what you create; let yourself create just for the fun and cathartic release of creative expression.

8 – Express

Music and art don't work for everyone as a means of self-expression. Some people do better through physical activity, like sports, running, or martial arts.

As you pass through the teenage years, you are processing an enormous amount of energy. Explore different ways to express that energy so it doesn't build up inside you and explode in ways that make you miserable.

Helpful
Hopeful
Proud
Important
Unique
Humble
Understanding
Receptive
Courageous
Daring
Passionate
Clever
Able
Attractive
Enthusiastic
Innocent
Playful
Hopeful
Honest
Helpful
Curious
Sensual
Caring
Clever
Confident
Flexible
Open
Wise
Responsible
Valuable
Honest
Patient
Tender
Powerful
Compassionate
Protective
Thoughtful
Nurturing
Tender
Decisive
Valuable
Imaginative
Generous
Appreciative
Innocent
Gentle
Open
Wise
Humble
Intuitive
Funny
Creative
Daring
Able
Strong
Intuitive
Able
Generous
Intelligent
Confident
Flexible
Enthusiastic
Caring
Understanding
Attentive
Determined
Wise
Affectionate
Brilliant
Connected
Expressive
Forgiving
Creative
Deserving
Gentle
Curious
Attentive
Funny
Secure
Innocent
Decisive
Trustworthy
Sensitive
Trusting
Adventurous
Enthusiastic
Accepting
Loyal
Worthy
Peaceful
Thoughtful
Playful
Sensual
Trusting
Spirited
Unique
Worthy
Strong
Brilliant
Caring
Patient
Able
Loyal
Daring
Humble
Tender
Worthy
Secure
Proud
Clever
Loyal
Patient
Unique
Flexible

9 – Core Values

As you try on new personality structures, you are developing core values. If you do not consciously choose what these values are, they will be based on whatever you are most often exposed to. These experiences will influence you at an unconscious level.

You have the power to take control of the values you develop by choosing to emulate those you admire. Watch people you like who speak to you at a deep level and imagine how they are in real life. Consider what they may think the important parts of life are and what qualities are essential for success. Ask yourself if those qualities feel right to you, and if so, how can you express them in your life.

10 – Nothing Personal

Don't take what others do personally. Most of the time people are lost in their own little world, so how they treat you has nothing to do with you; you just happen to be there.

Perhaps you've had a day when you were in a bad mood and someone in the hall bumped into you, so you yelled at them. If you had bumped into a wet floor marker, you probably would have yelled at it too.

So if someone flips out on you, realize they probably would have flipped out on whomever or whatever happened to be there at the time.

CAUTION
WET
FLOOR

11 – Shaving

Once you shave, the hair tends to grow thicker. When the hair starts sprouting everywhere, decide if you're ready to keep up with the maintenance of using a razor.

If you don't like your arm hair or the hairs on your toes, consider waxing or another method, because if you shave it, it will probably come back thicker and darker.

If you use a razor, get one that's only for you. Some personal grooming items, like razors and lip balm should not be shared.

12 – Waxing

Waxing hurts. You're ripping the hair out by the roots. When done correctly, the results can last for weeks.

If you're a do it yourself type, be careful not to burn yourself with the hot wax. Mineral oil and a paper towel will remove any wax that winds up where you don't want to pull it off with the paper strips … including the bathroom counter.

13 – Removal Cream

Hair removing creams smell bad. They are made from an acid which burns away the hair just above the root ball. The good news is they can make your skin soft. The dangerous part is they can easily burn you if you don't follow the directions.

Do NOT use them if you have any broken skin; the cream will make even a tiny scratch into a big cut that might leave a scar. For some reason, it seems to eat away the area around the broken skin, turning it into a much bigger abrasion.

14 – Pimples

Everyone – including adults – gets pimples. They are nothing to be ashamed of or embarrassed by. Although at times they may seem huge, extremely inconvenient, and sometimes even painful, pimples are simply one of the annoyances that are a part of life.

Pimples, like many of the other things that bug each of us in unique ways, will soon pass.

aarrghh

15 – Face Care

To help reduce the number and severity of pimples, use a gentle face cleanser and not body soap on your face. Body soap can dry out your face, and cause the glands under your skin to compensate by creating more oil.

It's never too early to start using moisturizer, especially on delicate facial skin. If you use it before you go outside, also apply sunscreen.

Love your skin; it protects you more than you realize.

16 – Don't Squeeze

Resist the temptation to squeeze pimples. If you squeeze them, you will break the skin and it will most likely leave a scar.

If the pimple is swollen and painful, gently press a warm wet facecloth against it several times a day for a minute or two. You can also try an ice cube inside a washcloth – don't put ice directly on skin because it will burn.

This is one of the many areas of life where we have to experiment to find what works for our situation.

17 – Acne Medication

Acne medication is an acid – be careful with it. Always test a small spot to make sure it doesn't burn your skin.

Some people are more sensitive to different types of acne medication. Read the ingredients to learn which ones work best for you. Follow the directions and apply it only to the pimples.

Many acne medications will also bleach towels and clothing. Wash your hands thoroughly after touching the medicine.

If your acne is severe and the products from the store do not help, see a dermatologist (a skin doctor) for guidance and possibly a prescription.

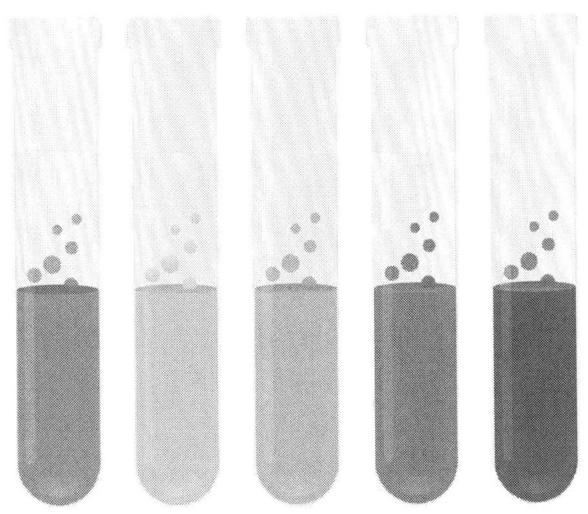

18 – Sweat

As a teenager, it's never too early to start using deodorant. Everyone's sweat stinks. That's why they make so many different brands of deodorant. If you get super sweaty under your arms, you may want to try one with an antiperspirant.

19 – Laundry

Have your parents show you how to use the washer and dryer, so your clothes are always clean. Dirty clothes worn by teenagers smell – bad. It's not just you; it's all your friends too.

Some of them may not admit it, but adults also get smelly, so perhaps you can offer to do a load of your parent's laundry while you're doing yours.

20 – Respect

Respect everyone, beginning with yourself. Some people say respect must be earned, but that doesn't make sense to me because why would someone give you respect if you don't respect them?

If you treat everyone with respect, then others tend to respect you in return.

If you respect yourself, you'll automatically work to find a way out of any situation in which you are being treated badly.

RESPECT
RESPECT
RESPECT
RESPECT
RESPECT
RESPECT
RESPECT
RESPECT
RESPECT
RESPECT

Honesty
is the best
Policy

21 – Honesty

If people are honest, we respect them even if we don't like what they are saying or doing.

When we are honest with ourselves, we create self-respect, even if we don't like what we've been saying or doing.

By cultivating self-respect, we begin to make decisions that honor ourselves. Through honoring ourselves, we begin to experience self-love.

When we love our own self, only then are we able to truly love others for who they are.

22 – Dating Age

As a teenager, hormonal changes can affect how we feel about others. These feelings can be very intense and confusing.

To stay out of legal and moral trouble, it's a good idea to date only people who are within a year or two of your age. If you're interested in someone outside of that range, wait until you are both at least 20 years old. If there's really a love connection there, it will still be there then and you can explore it as equal adults.

23 – Communicate

If you like someone, tell them. Chances are if they like you, they are just as nervous about telling you.

You can peek at each other across the room, whisper to your friends, and keep wondering, or you can walk up to him or her and say "I like you" or "I want to spend time with you." Either they will say they like you too, or they won't.

Do this when you are both alone. People sometimes get self-conscious and have a hard time being honest in front of their friends in these situations.

24 – Heart Pain

If you like someone and they don't like you back, it hurts. There's no way around that kind of pain. But knowing the feeling is not mutual allows you to grow past it. Be gentle with yourself and do things that make you feel good. Eventually your heart will move on and you'll like someone else.

25 – Moved On

Once you've moved on and found someone new to spend time with, there's a chance the first person you liked will suddenly want to be with you now that you're not interested.

Sometimes people only want what they can't have, and once they finally get it, they don't want it. People are really weird like that. Even full-grown adults do that. I don't know why.

26 – Sex

Wait to have sex until you are certain you are both ready. There is no need to rush. Don't let yourself be pressured into sex by anyone … not even by your own hormones.

Physical intimacy of any kind can unleash really big feelings, and it's OK if you're not ready. If you're uncertain, you're not ready.

Talk about it with each other, and respect each other's feelings. Some people wait to get married before having sex while others don't.

Also … Yes, you CAN get pregnant the first time, so discuss birth control BEFORE sex. If you're unable to talk about birth control, you're not ready for the intimacy of sex.

27 – Consent and Tea

Always ask for consent before touching someone. When it comes to sex and any kind of touching, no means NO.

It can be helpful to think of sex and touching like tea. Sometimes when a friend offers you tea, it sounds good. They might begin preparing the tea, and you change your mind. You are allowed to say no after you've said yes, even if the tea is already brewed. No one should ever force tea down your throat.

In the same way you would not try to give tea to someone who is not in a position to drink it on their own, you don't touch or try to have sex with someone who is not in a position to consent, even if they said yes before they passed out.

If you say no, stick with it for the rest of the date, even if that means ending the date early. Changing your mind after saying no makes everything very confusing for everyone. It's better to wait until another opportunity arises. That way you'll avoid any bitter aftertaste.

Remember, you or the other person can say no at any time, even if you've already started being physically intimate.

A yes can become a no, but a no means no. If someone tells you to stop, always respect it.

For more clarity on this issue, please watch "Tea and Consent" by the Thames Valley Police on YouTube: https://youtu.be/pZwvrxVavnQ

28 – Self Respect

You determine how others treat you by how you treat yourself. Respect yourself, be kind to yourself, and be honest with yourself. Without even thinking about it, people observe how you treat yourself, and then follow your lead.

29 – Sleep

Your cells are building a whole new body. Let it sleep so it can build. Remind your parents because they probably forgot how much sleep teenagers need.

30 – Eat and Move

Your body and mind need fuel and exercise as well as sleep. To help your body grow strong, feed yourself healthy food that makes you feel good.

Your body will appreciate it when you incorporate movement into your play: dance across the room, jump up and down when you play video games, get outside and run around, or do whatever movement feels fun and gets your heart pumping.

31 – Budget

Even though you're a teenager, learning how to create and maintain a budget is an important part of developing into a fully functional adult. This crucial life skill is not always taught in school.

Sometimes parents don't want their kids to know about the house budget because they are trying to protect you, or because they feel finances are private.

If your parents don't want to discuss the house budget, ask them to help you create a pretend budget. Or you can do a search online to learn how to set one up for yourself.

Research how much an apartment or house costs to rent, and collect the receipts from the grocery store to see how much the food you eat costs each week. Think about what else you may need to spend money on, like transportation and the things you do for fun. Then figure out how much you'll need to earn to cover your costs.

No matter what you do for work, knowing how to handle money effectively will help you for the rest of your life.

32 – Parents

Parents make mistakes, but they usually don't want their kids to know. If the kids knew, then the illusion that they are the all-powerful protector would be destroyed.

Some parents are never ready to give up their role as protector. When you catch your parent making a mistake, be gentle with them.

33 – Secure Your Own Oxygen Mask

On an airplane, they always tell you to secure your own oxygen mask before assisting others. This is true in life also.

Make sure you do what you need to do, whether it's homework or eating or resting or whatever it is you need to function, before helping others.

ASK

34 – Escaping Drama

Many people, and not just teenagers, get caught up in the things they want and the latest drama at school or work. This type of self-centered focus can make us feel isolated, insecure, and miserable.

Instead of being concerned about what you get and what others are doing, ask:

How can I help you today?

What can I give or do to be of service to others?

35 – Give What is Extra

Once you help and give to others, you'll discover it feels wonderful to give. However, you still have to take care of your own needs, so give what you have that is extra. When you take care of your own needs first, then you can continue to give without ever expecting anything in return. In this way, we can give freely, meaning it doesn't matter what the other person does with our gift because we have truly given it away.

There is a saying: one flame can light a thousand candles. Keep your flame lit so you can light up thousands of others.

36 – Time

Time is valuable, but you cannot save it nor can you earn it. You can only spend time, so spend it wisely on the things that are important to you, with your full attention.

When it's time to play, give yourself fully to play and have fun.

When it's time to do school work, give yourself fully to the work and be productive.

When it's time to rest, give yourself fully to resting and be refreshed.

37 – Meditation and Laughter

If you want to be happy no matter what is happening, cultivate your innate ability to meditate.

If you've ever laughed uncontrollably or been so absorbed in your activity you lost all sense of time and place, that's meditation.

Meditation is when the mind stops thinking and life becomes pure experience.

HERE
NOW
BREATH
BEING
BODY
THIS
BREATH
BEING
BODY
THIS
BREATH
BEING
BODY
Accepting
Openly
Listening
Experiencing
Following
Listening
Receptively

38 – Silence

Meditation can also be developed by spending time alone in silence. When done correctly, meditation will give energy and joy to your life.

While spontaneous meditation happens in the midst of activity, we can enter into meditation anytime by simply sitting still and focusing the mind on one point. With practice, the thoughts will slow down and finally stop.

If we practice sitting in silence, we'll be able to tap into silence anytime. We can draw upon our inner clarity by taking a minute to meditate before taking a test, before playing sports, and before reacting whenever we feel stressed.

39 – You Matter

You matter. Every person exerts an influence on others and on the world, whether or not that influence is acknowledged.

Even your basic physical presence changes the world; when the wind blows, the air flows around you, and thus alters the wind currents.

Don't ever believe that you don't make a difference, because no matter what you do, you make an impact on the world and everyone in your life.

40 – Mood Swings

Mood swings are normal.

Getting stuck in one mood is not. Sometimes we need to cry or spend some time alone or talk with a close friend to process complex emotions.

If you've become stuck in a dark mood for two weeks or longer, get help from a trusted adult.

If you don't find the help you need, keep looking. You deserve to be happy.

Pause

41 – Pause

Your mind is processing information at lightning speed. Allow your mind to stop once in a while.

A great gift to yourself is taking time to focus completely on your breathing for a full minute at least once each day.

42 – Choices

We make choices all day long, some are small like what clothes to wear and some are big, like deciding whether or not to go to a party.

Part of growing up is learning to accept the responsibility of making a decision.

Don't do anything just because other people are doing it. Stick to doing things because YOU have a reason for doing them that makes sense to you.

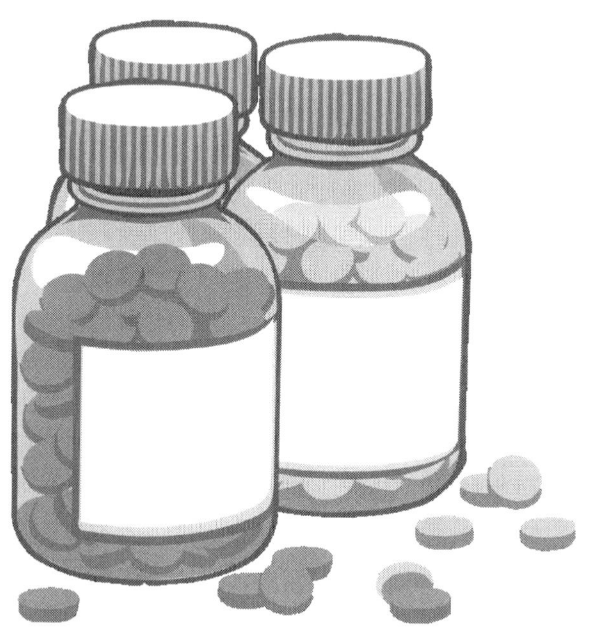

43 – Medication

Prescription medications can be just as dangerous, or sometimes even more dangerous, than illegal drugs. If you require medication, don't share it with anyone even if they ask.

Be careful with medications you can buy without a prescription. When you take a medication that you don't need, it can do harmful things to the body.

Sometimes these effects are permanent.

44 – Drugs

If you are curious about drugs, research them in detail. Don't believe everything you read on the Internet; instead take into account what site you're reading and what scientific studies they used to get their facts.

We all have different body chemistry, so how a drug affects you will be different than how it affects someone else, and how it affects an adult is different than what it does to a teenager.

Learn about the risks, and before you decide to put a drug into your body, make sure you can live with the worst effect it may have.

When it comes to the bad things in life, everyone thinks that it will never happen to them.

45 – Alcohol

Alcohol is a drug. It falls into the class called sedatives, which means it makes you sleepy and relaxes your inhibitions.

Inhibitions are what keep us from doing stupid things.

Some people's inhibitions are wound so tightly they are afraid to cross the street, while other people's inhibitions are so loose they run into traffic without looking. Most adults fall some place in between these two extremes.

In teenagers, the part of your brain that controls inhibitions has not fully developed. This means if you drink alcohol, you are more likely to do stupid things you will regret later.

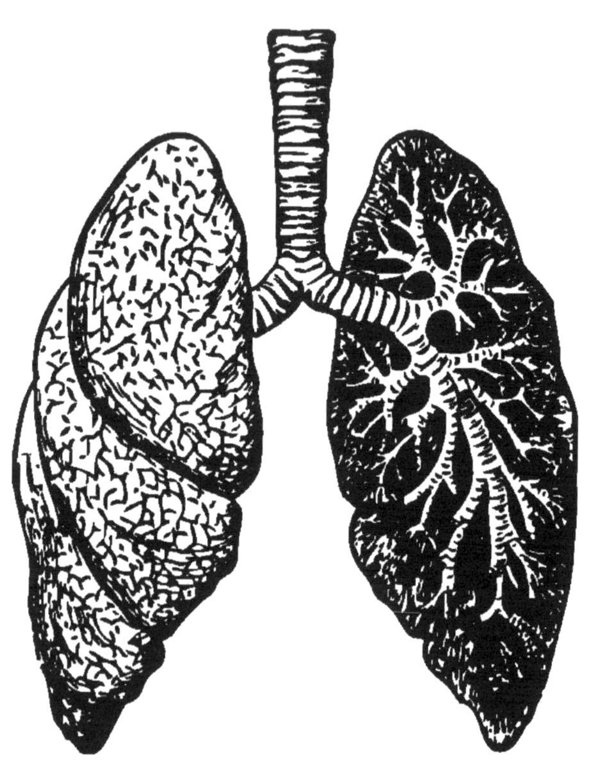

46 – Inhaling

Your lungs are built for inhaling air. They have this incredible ability to deliver oxygen immediately to the blood stream.

Anything else you suck in also goes straight into your blood stream, which is good news for people with asthma who cannot breathe without medication.

Other substances like cigarettes, vaporizers, and e-cigs can damage delicate lung tissue making it hard to breathe later on in life. It's always a good idea to be picky about what you choose to inhale.

47 – Pay Attention

Just like in real life, when you're hanging out with friends on social media or another Internet forum, pay attention to who is there.

If you're in a space that other teens normally visit, look around once in a while for any adults who don't belong. Point them out to your friends and keep each other safe.

trust yourself

48 – Instincts

Trust your instincts. When something feels wrong, it probably is.

Don't panic. Instead tell someone first.

Then cautiously investigate or go get help, and trust yourself.

49 – Getting Hurt

When you get hurt, whether it's physical or emotional, it helps to tell someone.

Just by letting someone know that you are hurt, the healing process begins. It is also OK to cry. Expressing pain through tears, words, and connection with others allows you to release the pain and heal faster.

This is true at any age.

50 – Peer Pressure

At a very basic, primal level, we all want to belong. This is why peer pressure can feel so strong.

There will be times when we need to be brave and stand apart. Doing what we know is right is always more important than belonging to the group. Again, trust yourself.

51 – The Bully

A bully at any age is a frightened lonely person. They don't know how to ask for what they need, so they push other people around.

If a bully comes after you, or if you see someone being bullied, stand up to them and have compassion for them.

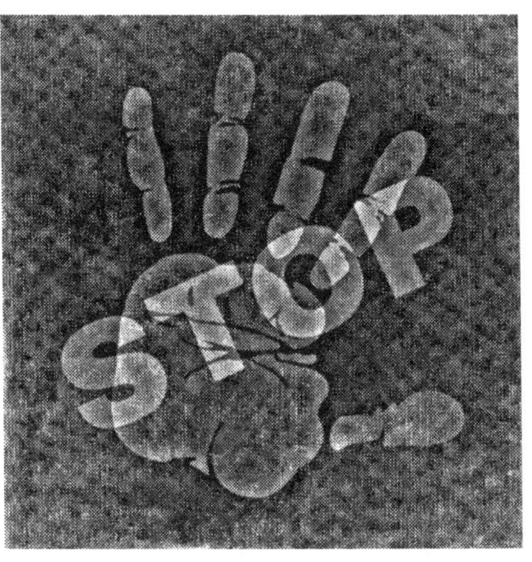

A bully usually doesn't even realize how much pain they are in, especially when they are a teenager. They are angry and confused. You cannot fix them, or anyone else, but you can treat them with kindness and firm boundaries.

52 – Unique Qualities

Not everyone or everything fits neatly into a category. Celebrate the ways in which you don't fit.

Sometimes it is in big ways. Other times there are little differences. These are your unique qualities and they are awesome.

53 – Friendships

It's normal for friendships to change over time. Some may grow deeper, while other friendships may fade into the background. This happens naturally as interests and activities change. However, all friendships need care and attention for them to survive.

When you are deciding who to spend time with, ask yourself which friends make you feel the most free.

With so many internal shifts happening, it can be difficult to pick which friendships are worth cultivating. Best friends bring out the best in one another.

Together, these friendships form a personal tribe that become a source of fun and laughter, as well as a support to help you through any challenges you face.

To help you discover who are the friends in your tribe, ask yourself:

- When you are around them, do you like yourself?
- Can you share your thoughts and feelings with them?
- Do you feel relaxed and open when you see them?

These are the best types of people to be around … choose them whenever you can.

54 – Learning to Drive

Learning to drive is challenging; teaching someone to drive is even tougher. Be prepared for frustration from both yourself and your teacher when you head out on the road.

55 – Car Power

Driving feels great! Having a 2,000 pound piece of machinery respond to your foot and hand creates an immense sense of power.

You can flatten almost anything that you drive over; however what doesn't get crushed will cause your vehicle to squish you. Respect that power each and every time you drive.

If you are distracted – by anything – stop in a parking spot until you can refocus your mind on driving.

56 – Driving Reaction

Driving is more than a rational act. It involves more than knowing what pedal does what and where to look when. Through experience we develop a felt-sense of what is going on with and around the vehicle.

There is way too much happening to think through every move you need to make. Instead you have to learn to rely on your felt-sense and trust your hands and feet will react in the right way at the right time.

This can be learned only by practicing and paying close attention to what you and others are doing every time you drive.

57 – Ask Questions

Asking questions – lots of them – is a great way to grow. As a teenager, you're not expected to know everything. You are expected to be old enough to ask about the things you need to know.

Questions are never foolish. Don't ever let anyone – including yourself – make you think they are.

If you're not getting the answers you need, try asking the question in a different way.

58 – Be Kind

The world can feel harsh sometimes, so it's a good idea to always be kind, especially when you don't want to be.

Kindness is a special type of super power that helps in every situation.

When you are kind to others, it creates a sense of connection, and this sense of connection feels wonderful, even when sad things happen.

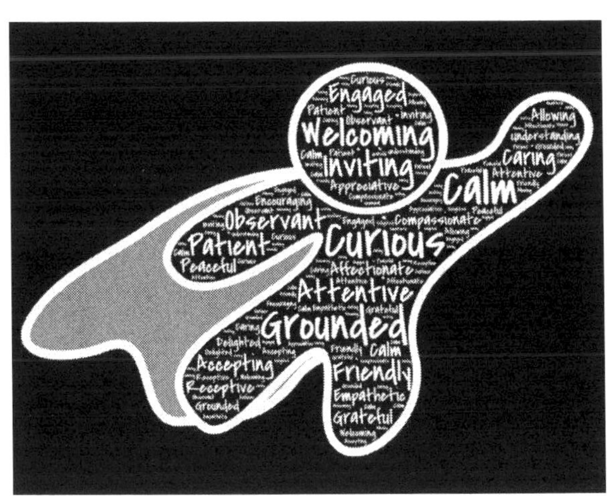
Curious
Engaged
Patient
Observant
Welcoming
Inviting
Calm
Appreciative
Allowing
understanding
Caring
Attentive
Calm
Encouraging
Observant
Compassionate
Patient
Curious
Peaceful
Affectionate
Attentive
Grounded
Delighted
Accepting
Friendly
Calm
Receptive
Friendly
Empathetic
Grounded
Grateful
Welcoming

59 – Smile Power

Sometimes something as simple as a smile can change a person's entire world.

Smiling at yourself in the mirror before you leave and when you get home can change your mood for the better too. It might even make you laugh!

Experiment and discover for yourself if this is true.

60 – Little by Little

All the little things add up.

If we eat a little bit over and over, our stomach gets full.

If we work at learning something little by little, it sticks in our mind.

If we do some little thing over and over, it becomes part of our habits.

The good news is, we all have the power to choose the little things we do wisely.

IMPORTANT

61 – What's Important

We always do what we *think* we want to do. This is a wonderful thing, as it keeps us honest.

We can always look at our actions to discover what we think is important.

We can then take this information to see if what we think is important matches up to what we *feel* is important.

If it doesn't, we can make adjustments to our thinking as necessary, and our actions will follow.

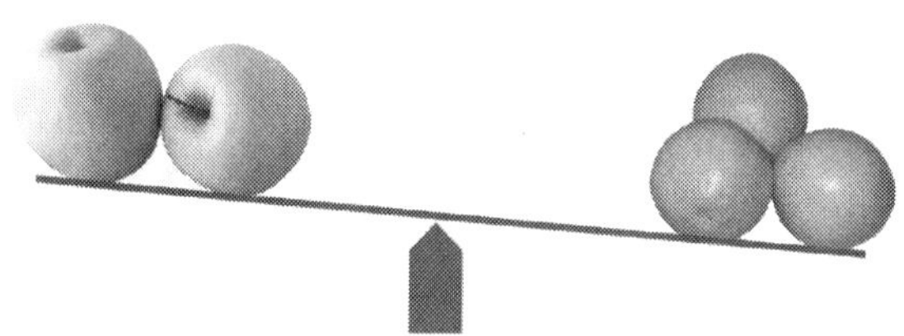

62 – No Comparison

It's natural for us to want to compare ourselves to others, but it doesn't really give us any useful information.

There is only one of each of us, so it's like trying to compare an apple to an orange – they're both fruit and tasty, but there's too many differences to say one is better than the other.

Look to other people for inspiration, but know you are unique and will do things in your own way.

Instead of trying to measure up to something outside of yourself, concentrate on doing what no one else can: being the best version of you today.

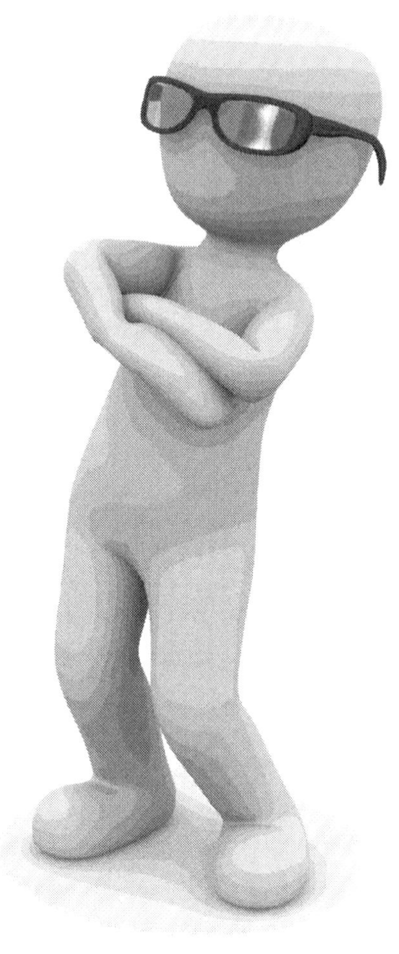

63 – Be Cool

Being cool is being comfortable in your own skin, even when you're not. This doesn't mean you go numb. It means you are comfortable with your own uncomfortableness.

64 – Happy

No one ever needs a reason to be happy.

When we are sad or angry or upset in any way, there is always a reason if we look deeply enough. However, when we're happy, we're often happy simply because we're happy.

Many adults have forgotten this important fact of life, but you don't have to forget.

Bliss is our natural state. It is your perfect right to be filled with joy for absolutely no reason at all.

ABOUT THE AUTHOR

Jenna Sundell is a Buddhist monk who enjoys sharing her spiritual practice of meditation and mindfulness and her perspective on life. She teaches mainly adults because they have forgotten what kids already know: we are boundless Joy.

Once you turn 18, you can sit with her at Dharma Center in San Diego if you would like to learn more. She also shares Buddhist teachings through her blog and other books she has written. She visits the wacky world of social media from time to time. If it's OK with your parents, you can find her at: Facebook.com/JennaSundellAuthor and Twitter @jennasundell.

www.dharmacenter.com

www.jennasundell.com

Made in the USA
San Bernardino, CA
09 March 2019